Descendants of Joseph Bell

Generation 1

1.   JOSEPH[1] BELL was born about 1818 in England. He died before 01 Jan 1866 in Scotland. He married Elizabeth McLachlan, daughter of Hugh McLachlan on 10 May 1840 in Glasgow, Lanarkshire, Scotland. She was born about 1817 in Lanarkshire, Scotland. She died before 01 Jan 1866 in Scotland.

More About Joseph Bell:

Living In: 1841 With his father in law at Gibson St. 3, Glasgow St. James, Lanarkshire, Scotland.

Living In: 1851 20 Warrenstone Close, Edinburgh High Church Parish, Midlothian County, Scotland.

Occupation: 1841 in Glasgow St. James, Lanarkshire, Scotland; Blacksmith

Occupation: 1851 in Edinburgh High Church Parish, Midlothian County, Scotland; Blacksmith and Chain Maker

Joseph Bell and Elizabeth McLachlan had the following children:

      i.   GEORGE[2] BELL was born about 1841 in Glasgow, Lanarkshire, Scotland.

3.   ii. WILLIAM BELL was born on 16 May 1845 in Glasgow, Lanarkshire, Scotland. He died on 18 Mar 1924 in Coalgate, Oklahoma. He married Ann Kirkwood Patterson, daughter of Robert Patterson and Barbara Speirs on 01 Jan 1866 in Carnbuslang, Lanarkshire, Scotland. She was born on 15 May 1846 in Silverbanks,Cambuslang, Lanarkshire, Scotland. She died on 07 Jan 1934 in Coalgate, Oklahoma.

      iii.   JOSEPH BELL was born about 1849 in Glasgow, Lanarkshire, Scotland.

Generation 2

2.   WILLIAM[2] BELL (Joseph[1]) was born on 16 May 1845 in Glasgow, Lanarkshire, Scotland. He died on 18 Mar 1924 in Coalgate, Oklahoma. He married Ann Kirkwood Patterson, daughter of Robert Patterson and Barbara Speirs on 01 Jan 1866 in Carnbuslang, Lanarkshire, Scotland. She was born on 15 May 1846 in Silverbanks,Cambuslang, Lanarkshire, Scotland. She died on 07 Jan 1934 in Coalgate, Oklahoma.

More About William Bell:

Burial: 20 Mar 1924 in Coalgate Cemetery, Coalgate, Oklahoma

Immigration: Mar 1869 in From Scotland to Maryland

Occupation: 1866 in Cambuslang, Lanarkshire, Scotland; Coal Miner

Occupation: 07 Jul 1870 in Election District number 16, Allegany County, Maryland; Miner

Occupation: 1879 in Krebs, Indian Territory (Present Day Oklahoma); Coal Miner

Occupation: 1900 in Coalgate, Choctaw Nation, Indian Territory (Present Day Oklahoma); Coal Miner

Occupation: 1910 in Coalgate, Oklahoma; Retired

Occupation: 1920 in Coalgate, Oklahoma; Retired

More About Ann Kirkwood Patterson:

Burial: 09 Jan 1934 in Coalgate Cemetery, Coalgate, Oklahoma

Immigration: 22 Jul 1871 Arrived in New York, New York on ship "India"

Living In: 02 Apr 1871 Ann and her children are living with her parents in Silverbanks, Cambuslang, Lanarkshire, Scotland.

Living In: Jun 1880 Delta, Keokuk County, Iowa

Living In: 1930 Coalgate, Coal County, Oklahoma

Notes for Ann Kirkwood Patterson:

Headstone has May 16, 1846 for date of birth.

William Bell and Ann Kirkwood Patterson had the following children:

3.   i. BARBARA PATTERSON[3] BELL was born on 03 Mar 1867 in Silverbanks, Cambuslang, Lanarkshire, Scotland. She died on 12 Mar 1936 in Oklahoma City, Oklahoma. She married ALEXANDER BOWIE. He was born about 22 Dec 1858 in Pennsylvania. He died on 04 Mar 1889 in McAlester, Indian Territory (Present Day Oklahoma). She married (2) ROBERT H. BROWN on 13 Sep 1893 in Thurber, Erath County, Texas. He was born on 08 May 1867 in Scotland. He died on 25 Dec 1950 in St Louis, Missouri.

         ii. JOSEPH BELL was born on 22 Mar 1869 in Dalserf, Lanarkshire, Scotland. He died on 08 May 1882 in Indian Territory (Present Day Oklahoma).

More About Joseph Bell:
Burial: McAlester Cemetery, McAlester, Oklahoma

4.   iii. WILLIAM BELL was born in 1872 in Maryland. He died in 1954 in Illinois. He married (1) MARGARET KERR, daughter of Thomas Kerr about 1893. She was born on 08 Jul 1873 in Scotland. She died on 17 Mar 1921 in Collinsville, Illinois. He married (2) ROSE KAUFMAN about 1923. She was born on 30 Aug 1890 in Carlinville, Illinois. She died in Jan 1980 in Alton, Madison County, Illinois.

         iv. ROBERT H. BELL was born on 08 Sep 1874 in Maryland. He died on 07 Nov 1902. He married Mary M. Boozle on 16 May 1897 in Muscogee County, Indian Territory, (present day Oklahoma).

More About Robert H. Bell:
Burial: Coalgate Cemetery, Coalgate, Oklahoma
Occupation: 1900 in Madrid, Santa Fe County, New Mexico; Coal Miner

Notes for Robert H. Bell:
1900 U.S. census shows Robert was married about 1897 and still married in 1900. He was living as a boarder in 1900.

5.   v. ELIZABETH BELL was born in Aug 1879 in Iowa. She died on 11 Aug 1960 in Coalgate, Oklahoma. She married John McInnis, son of John McInnes and Mary Belle VanBrocklin in Feb 1902 in Coalgate, Choctaw Nation, Indian Territory (Present Day Oklahoma). He was born on 15 Dec 1878 in Ohio. He died on 20 Aug 1918 in Coalgate, Oklahoma.

6.   vi. JAMES P. BELL was born on 17 Dec 1880 in Iowa. He died in Aug 1966 in Oklahoma. He married Isabel Liddle on 05 Jun 1909 in Coalgate, Coal County, Oklahoma. She was born about 1886 in Indian Territory (Present Day Oklahoma).

7.   vii. JOSEPH BELL was born on 13 Jun 1883 in Krebs, Indian Territory (Present Day Oklahoma). He died on 27 Oct 1958 in Coalgate, Oklahoma. He married Emily Louise Connally, daughter of Charles Clay Connaly and Willie Etta Jenkins on 18 Nov 1906 in Choctaw Nation, Indian Territory (Present Day Oklahoma). She was born on 10 Aug 1885 in Huntsville, Alabama. She died on 07 Oct 1951 in Coalgate, Oklahoma.

8.   viii. GEORGE PATTERSON BELL was born on 07 May 1886 in Krebs, Indian Territory

(Oklahoma). He died on 04 Sep 1949 in Gorman, Texas. He married Blanche Lee Hanlin on 26 Feb 1907 in Coalgate, Choctaw Nation, Indian Territory (Present Day Oklahoma). She was born on 06 Mar 1887 in Mississippi. She died on 27 Jan 1963 in Oklahoma.

Generation 3

3. BARBARA PATTERSON[3] BELL (William[2], Joseph[1]) was born on 03 Mar 1867 in Silverbanks, Cambuslang, Lanarkshire, Scotland. She died on 12 Mar 1936 in Oklahoma City, Oklahoma. She married ALEXANDER BOWIE. He was born about 22 Dec 1858 in Pennsylvania. He died on 04 Mar 1889 in McAlester, Indian Territory (Present Day Oklahoma). She married (2) ROBERT H. BROWN on 13 Sep 1893 in Thurber, Erath County, Texas. He was born on 08 May 1867 in Scotland. He died on 25 Dec 1950 in St Louis, Missouri.

More About Barbara Patterson Bell:
Burial: 15 Mar 1936 in Coalgate Cemetery, Coalgate, Oklahoma
Immigration: 22 Jul 1871 in Arrived in New York, New York on ship "India"

Notes for Barbara Patterson Bell:
Headstone has February 24, 1868 for date of birth.

More About Alexander Bowie:
Burial: North McAlester Cemetery, McAlester, Oklahoma

Alexander Bowie and Barbara Patterson Bell had the following child:

9.   i. ANNIE BELL[4] BOWIE was born on 11 Mar 1886 in Krebs, Indian Territory (Present Day Oklahoma). She died on 31 Jan 1978 in Amarillo, Potter County, Texas. She married Claude Ray Badgett, son of James Royal Badgett and Mary Belle Wakefield on 16 Apr 1902 in Coalgate, Choctaw Nation, Indian Territory (Present Day Oklahoma). He was born on 27 Jan 1881 in Kentuckytown, Grayson County, Texas. He died on 18 Apr 1960 in Plainview, Texas.

More About Robert H. Brown:
Burial: 29 Dec 1950 in Coalgate Cemetery, Coalgate, Oklahoma
Living In: 1935 Oklahoma City, Oklahoma
Occupation: 1900 in Coalgate, Choctaw Nation, Indian Territory (Present Day Oklahoma); Coal Miner
Occupation: 1910 in Coalgate, Coal County, Oklahoma; Coal Mine Fire Boss
Occupation: 1920 in Coalgate, Coal County, Oklahoma; Miner
Occupation: 1930 in Coalgate, Coal County, Oklahoma; District Inspector of Coal Mines
Occupation: Bet. 1931-1947; Chief Mine Inspector for Oklahoma
Occupation: 1940 in Oklahoma City, Oklahoma; State Mine Inspector

Notes for Robert H. Brown:
Arrived in United States from Scotland in 1881.

Robert H. Brown and Barbara Patterson Bell had the following children:

          i. AGNES[4] BROWN was born on 25 Jun 1894 in Indian Territory (Present Day Oklahoma). She died in Jun 1981 in Fort Smith, Arkansas. She married S. O. HENSHAW.

         ii. ELIZABETH BROWN was born in Apr 1898 in Indian Territory (Present Day

Oklahoma).

More About Elizabeth Brown:
Living In: Bet. 1920-1940 Living with her parents.
Occupation: 1920 in Coalgate, Coal County, Oklahoma; School Teacher
Occupation: 1930 in Coalgate, Coal County, Oklahoma; Public School Teacher
Occupation: 1940 in Oklahoma City, Oklahoma; Deputy County Clerk

10. iii. WILLIAM BROWN was born on 07 Feb 1900 in Indian Territory (Present Day Oklahoma). He died on 04 Apr 1982 in Krebs, Oklahoma. He married (UNKNOWN).

 iv. REGINA BROWN was born on 28 Jun 1903 in Indian Territory (Present Day Oklahoma). She died in Oct 1986 in Fort Smith, Arkansas. She married (UNKNOWN) BOOTH.

 v. ROBERT BROWN was born about Feb 1909 in Oklahoma.

Notes for Robert Brown:
Robert is only seen on the 1910 U.S. census for Coalgate, Oklahoma.

4. **WILLIAM**[3] **BELL** (William[2], Joseph[1]) was born in 1872 in Maryland. He died in 1954 in Illinois. He married (1) **MARGARET KERR**, daughter of Thomas Kerr about 1893. She was born on 08 Jul 1873 in Scotland. She died on 17 Mar 1921 in Collinsville, Illinois. He married (2) **ROSE KAUFMAN** about 1923. She was born on 30 Aug 1890 in Carlinville, Illinois. She died in Jan 1980 in Alton, Madison County, Illinois.

More About William Bell:
Burial: Bethalto United Methodist Church Cemetery, Bethalto, Illinois
Occupation: 1900 in Precinct 10, Las Animas County, Colorado; Coal Miner
Occupation: 1910 in Collinsville, Madison County, Illinois; Coal Miner
Occupation: 1920 in Collinsville, Madison County, Illinois; Coal Miner
Occupation: 1930 in Bethalto, Madison County, Illinois; Coal Miner

Notes for William Bell:
In 1900 William was working in Las Animas County, Colorado while Margaret was living in Cerrillos, New Mexico with their children.

More About Margaret Kerr:
Burial: 20 Mar 1921 in St. John Cemetery, Collinsville, Illinois
Living In: 1900 Cerrilos, Santa Fe County, New Mexico

Notes for Margaret Kerr:
Margaret was living, with her children, in Cerrillos, New Mexico in 1900 while William was working in Las Animas County, Colorado.

William Bell and Margaret Kerr had the following children:
 i. WILLIAM[4] BELL was born on 28 Sep 1894 in Coalgate, Choctaw Nation, Indian Territory (Present Day Oklahoma).

More About William Bell:
Occupation: 1910 in Collinsville, Madison County, Illinois; Drug Salesman
Occupation: 1917 in Detroit, Michigan; Street Car Conductor

ii.   AGNES BELL was born on 29 Jul 1897 in Madrid, New Mexico. She died on 22 Feb 1938 in Belleville, Sr. Clair County, Illinois. She married HARRY NAY. He was born on 13 Aug 1898 in Illinois. He died in Sep 1983 in Illinois.

More About Agnes Bell:
Burial: 25 Feb 1938 in St. John Cemetery, Collinsville Madison County, Illinois
Living In: 1920 Living with her parents in Collinsville, Illinois.
Living In: 1938 Collinsville, Madison County, Illinois
Occupation: 1920 in Collinsville, Madison County, Illinois; Clerk in Railroad Office

iii.   JOHN V. BELL was born in Feb 1899 in New Mexico.

More About John V. Bell:
Occupation: 1920 in Collinsville, Madison County, Illinois; Clerk in Railroad Office

More About Rose Kaufman:
Burial: Bethalto United Methodist Church Cemetery, Bethalto, Illinois

5.   ELIZABETH³ BELL (William², Joseph¹) was born in Aug 1879 in Iowa. She died on 11 Aug 1960 in Coalgate, Oklahoma. She married John McInnis, son of John McInnes and Mary Belle VanBrocklin in Feb 1902 in Coalgate, Choctaw Nation, Indian Territory (Present Day Oklahoma). He was born on 15 Dec 1878 in Ohio. He died on 20 Aug 1918 in Coalgate, Oklahoma.

More About Elizabeth Bell:
Burial: 14 Aug 1960 in Coalgate Cemetery, Coalgate, Oklahoma
Occupation: 1900 in Coalgate, Choctaw Nation, Indian Territory (Present Day Oklahoma); Saleswoman in Drugstore
Occupation: 1920 in Coalgate, Coal County, Oklahoma; Saleswoman in Drugstore
Occupation: 1930 in Coalgate, Coal County, Oklahoma; Retail Dry Goods Saleswoman

Notes for Elizabeth Bell:
Elizabeth McInnis Claimed by death at Home. Services for Elizabeth McInnis were held at the First Methodist church at 2 o'clock Sunday afternoon by Daniel Forbes, Mrs. McInnis and her husband, John McInnis, came to Coalgate 66 years ago from Krebs, and he preceded her in death 42 years ago, She died quietly at sleep at her home here Thursday. Mrs. McInnis worked for many years in the Corner Drug store and Margaret Covington's ready to wear store here. She was active in the Coalgate Garden Club. Linger Longer Embroidery Club, and the order of the Eastern Star. Surviving are two sons, C. R, McInnis, R. M. McInnis, and a daughter, Mrs. Peggy Helvey, one brother, Jim Bell of Henrietta, five grandchildren, and five great grandchildren. Pall bearers were W. E. Larecy, W. H. Bailey, Eddie Cox, Arthur Pope, Jim Farrimond, and Elmo Childers. Among the out of town relatives attending the services were Mrs. Agnes Hinshaw and Jean Booth of Ft. Smith, Ark; Mr. and Mrs. Billy Bell and daughter, and Bobbie Jean McInnis of Oklahoma City; Louise Sugar of Londoner, MD, Mrs. George Bell of Oklahoma City; Emma Doris Wyche of Durant, Jean Patterson and Annie Mowatt of Oklahoma City; Bob Patterson, John Hall and daughter of Henrietta; Mr. and Mrs. John Jones, Mrs. Ted Henderson of Wapanucha; Mrs. Harry Miller and granddaughter, Cynthia, Mrs. Ethel Harwell of Ada; Sam Covington, Mr. & Mrs. Bill Cowan of
Oklahoma City. Burial was at Coalgate cemetery with Slater funeral home directing.

More About John McInnis:
Burial: Coalgate Cemetery, Coalgate, Oklahoma
Occupation: 1900 in Coalgate, Choctaw Nation, Indian Territory (Present Day
Oklahoma); Bookkeeper
Occupation: 1910 in Coalgate, Coal County, Oklahoma; Livery Stable Prioprietor

Notes for John McInnis:
Headstone has last name spelled McInnis.

John McInnis and Elizabeth Bell had the following children:

11.   i. ROBERT J.[4] MCINNIS was born on 08 Aug 1905 in Coalgate, Oklahoma. He died on 07 Jul 1964 in Coalgate, Oklahoma. He married BILLYE PAULINE BLACK. She was born on 20 Apr 1911 in Oklahoma. She died on 12 Aug 1988.

12.   ii. CLAUD RAY MCINNIS was born on 24 Oct 1907 in Indian Territory (Present Day Oklahoma). He died on 22 Dec 1980. He married Katherine Marie Maloney on 31 Jul 1945 in Weatherford, Texas. She was born on 17 Feb 1913 in Texas. She died on 11 Oct 1992 in Dallas, Texas.

     iii. ANNABELL MCINNIS was born in 1911 in Oklahoma. She married (UNKNOWN) HELVEY.

6.   JAMES P.[3] BELL (William[2], Joseph[1]) was born on 17 Dec 1880 in Iowa. He died in Aug 1966 in Oklahoma. He married Isabel Liddle on 05 Jun 1909 in Coalgate, Coal County, Oklahoma. She was born about 1886 in Indian Territory (Present Day Oklahoma).

More About James P. Bell:
Living In: 1930 As a boarder in Detroit, Michigan.
Living In: 1966 Henryetta, Oklahoma
Occupation: 1900 in Coalgate, Choctaw Nation, Indian Territory (Present Day Oklahoma); Coal Miner
Occupation: 1910 in Coalgate, Oklahoma; Coal Miner
Occupation: 1918 in Henryetta, Oklahoma; Working for Blackstone Coal Mine in Henryetta, Oklahoma
Occupation: 1920 in Henryetta, Oklahoma; Coal Miner
Occupation: 1930 in Detroit, Michigan; Factory Worker
Occupation: 1940 in Henryetta, Oklahoma; Field Representative for Coal Company

Notes for James P. Bell:

World War One draft registration gives December 17, 1879 as date of birth. Social Security death index gives December 17, 1880 as date of birth. James is not on 1880 U.S. census taken June 22, 1880 in Iowa. World War Two draft registration gives date of birth as December 17, 1880.

More About Isabel Liddle:
Living In: 1930 Henryetta. Oklahoma

Notes for Isabel Liddle:
First name is Isabel on marriage certificate.

James P. Bell and Isabel Liddle had the following children:

13. i. ALICE LOVERE[4] BELL was born on 26 Dec 1909 in Oklahoma. She died on 28 Feb 1959 in Mount Vernon, Knox County, Ohio. She married RAYMOND L. BENTON. He was born on 25 Feb 1905. He died on 26 May 1976 in Mount Vernon, Knox County, Ohio.

 ii. ANNA MAE BELL was born about 1916 in Oklahoma.

 iii. JAMES P. BELL was born on 23 May 1922 in Oklahoma. He died on 07 Jul 1953 in Mediterranean Sea.

More About James P. Bell:
Burial: 29 Sep 1953 in Arlington National Cemetery Cause Of Death: Aircraft Crash
Military Service: Bet. July 1, 1943 -July 7, 1953, United States Marine Corps

Notes for James P. Bell:
Died in an aircraft crash while serving in the Marine Corps on the Mediterranean Sea. Served in World War Two and the Korean War as a fighter pilot. Rank at time of death was Major.

The President of the United States of America takes pleasure in presenting the Distinguished Flying Cross to Captain James P. Bell (MCSN: 0-29498), United States Marine Corps, for heroism while participating in aerial flight as a pilot attached to a Marine Aircraft Group from 19 September to November 1950. Captain Bell successfully completed his first through thirty-fifth combat mission in support of our ground forces, destroying and inflicting great damage to concentrations of North Korean vehicles, material and personnel. By his airmanship and devotion to duty in the face of enemy anti-aircraft fire, he contributed materially to the success of our troops. His conduct throughout was in keeping with the highest traditions of the United States Naval Service.
General Orders: Commanding General 1st Marine Aircraft Wing: Serial: 3864 (April 28, 1951)
Action Date: September 19 - November
1950 Service: Marine Corps
Rank: Captain

Citation dated

April 28, 1951

The President of the United States of America takes pleasure in presenting a Gold Star in lieu of a Second Award of the Distinguished Flying Cross to Captain James P. Bell (MCSN: 0-29498), United States Marine Corps, for extraordinary achievement while participating in aerial flight as a pilot of a fighter plane against the enemy on 6 June 1951. Captain Bell while leading a four plane flight on a close air support mission east of the Kweach'on Reservoir in Korea, worked in conjunction with a Marine Ground Controller whose progress was being held up by several hundred Chinese Communist troops. In spite of intense small arms fire and extremely adverse weather conditions, Captain Bell repeatedly led his flight in attacking entrenched enemy troops at minimum altitude with napalm, rockets and strafing. These successful attacks enabled the United Nations forces to occupy this important objective with negligible opposition. Three hundred dead enemy were confirmed by the occupying forces. With unerring judgment and outstanding

airmanship, Captain Bell dealt a damaging blow to the enemy. In so doing his alertness and efficient actions were in keeping with the highest traditions of the United States Naval Service.
General Orders: Commanding General 1st Marine Aircraft Wing: Serial: 6672 (July 21, 1951)
Action Date: June 6,
1951 Service: Marine
Corps Rank: Captain

Citation dated

July 21, 1951

----

     iv.   WILLIAM DAVID BELL was born about 1925 in Oklahoma.

7.   JOSEPH^3 BELL (William^2, Joseph^1) was born on 13 Jun 1883 in Krebs, Indian Territory (Present Day Oklahoma). He died on 27 Oct 1958 in Coalgate, Oklahoma. He married Emily Louise Connally, daughter of Charles Clay Connaly and Willie Etta Jenkins on 18 Nov 1906 in Choctaw Nation, Indian Territory (Present Day Oklahoma). She was born on 10 Aug 1885 in Huntsville, Alabama. She died on 07 Oct 1951 in Coalgate, Oklahoma.

More About Joseph Bell:
Burial: 30 Oct 1958 in Coalgate, Oklahoma
Occupation: 1900 in Coalgate, Choctaw Nation, Indian Territory (Present Day Oklahoma); Coal Miner
Occupation: 1910 in Coalgate, Coal County, Oklahoma; Pharmacist in Drug Store
Occupation: 1920 in Coalgate, Coal County, Oklahoma; Drug Store Proprietor
Occupation: 1930 in Coalgate, Coal County, Oklahoma; Druggist in Retail Drug Store
Occupation: 1940 in Coalgate, Coal County, Oklahoma; Druggist in Drug Store

Notes for Joseph Bell:
Owned his own drugstore in Coalgate, Oklahoma.
Funeral Record gives birth date as June 13, 1882. Headstone gives year of birth as 1882.
World War One and World War Two draft registrations give date of birth as June 13, 1883.
Marriage record indicates birth year of 1883.

More About Emily Louise Connally:
Burial: 09 Oct 1951 in Coalgate Cemetery, Coalgate, Oklahoma, Rev. Frank Warnke officiating
Occupation: 1940 in Coalgate, Coal County, Oklahoma; Assistant in Drug Store

Joseph Bell and Emily Louise Connally had the following children:

    i.   LOUISE H.^{4} BELL was born on 01 Dec 1907 in Oklahoma. She died on 18 Dec 1988 in Kaufman County, Texas. She married LEE SHUGAR. He was born about 1905. She married (2) LEO K. HUGHES on 26 Jan 1929 in Durant, Bryan County, Oklahoma. He was born about 1905.

        More About Louise H. Bell:
        Burial: Saint Paul Cemetery, Saint Paul, Texas

    ii.   JOSEPH CONNALLY BELL was born on 26 Oct 1910 in Coalgate, Oklahoma. He died on 21 Sep 1979 in Las Vegas, Nevada.

More About Joseph Connally Bell:
Burial: Woodlawn Cemetery, Las Vegas, Nevada
Military Service: Enlisted in U.S. Army at Los Angeles, California on November 20, 1943

14.   iii.   WILLIAM ROBERT BELL was born on 13 Jul 1922 in Coalgate, Oklahoma. He died on 4 Nov 1981 in Texas. He married Alma Louise Akerman, daughter of Donald Akerman and Theresa Diester on 11 Aug 1951 in McAllister, Oklahoma. She was born on 11 Nov 1930 in Sacred Heart, Oklahoma. She died on 22 Dec 2010 in Dallas, Texas.

8.   **GEORGE PATTERSON**[3] **BELL** (William[2], Joseph[1]) was born on 07 May 1886 in Krebs, Indian Territory (Oklahoma). He died on 04 Sep 1949 in Gorman, Texas. He married Blanche Lee Hanlin on 26 Feb 1907 in Coalgate, Choctaw Nation, Indian Territory (Present Day Oklahoma). She was born on 6 Mar 1887 in Mississippi. She died on 27 Jan 1963 in Oklahoma.

More About George Patterson Bell:
Burial: 06 Sep 1949 in Coalgate Cemetery, Coalgate, Oklahoma
Living In: 1940 George and Blanche are living with their son in law and daughter in Hugo, Oklahoma.
Occupation: 1910 in Hobart, Kiowa County, Oklahoma; Sewing Machine Agent
Occupation: 1916 in Okmulgee, Okmulgee County, Oklahoma; Coal Miner
Occupation: 1920 in Okmulgee, Okmulgee County, Oklahoma; Clerk in Loan Office
Occupation: 1930 in Oklahoma City, Oklahoma; Lease and Royalty Prosessor
Occupation: 1940 in Hugo, Choctaw County, Oklahoma; Independant Oil Lease Processor
Occupation: 1942 in Hugo, Choctaw County, Oklahoma; Self Employed
Occupation: 1949 in Hugo, Choctaw County, Oklahoma; Oil Lease Broker

More About Blanche Lee Hanlin:
Burial: Coalgate Cemetery, Coalgate, Oklahoma

Notes for Blanche Lee Hanlin:
Social Security death index gives year of death as 1963. Headstone gives year of death as 1962.

George Patterson Bell and Blanche Lee Hanlin had the following children:

     i. EMMA DORIS[4] BELL was born in 1908 in Oklahoma. She died in 1979. She married Ray L. Primo about 1928. He was born in 1905 in Missouri. He died in 1956.

     More About Emma Doris Bell:
     Burial: Coalgate Cemetery, Coalgate, Oklahoma

     ii.   WILLIAM BELL was born in Jan 1910 in Oklahoma.

Generation 4

9.   **ANNIE BELL**[4] **BOWIE** (Barbara Patterson[3] Bell, William[2] Bell, Joseph[1] Bell) was born on 11 Mar 1886 in Krebs, Indian Territory (Present Day Oklahoma). She died on 31 Jan 1978 in Amarillo, Potter County, Texas. She married Claude Ray Badgett, son of James Royal Badgett and Mary Belle Wakefield on 16 Apr 1902 in Coalgate, Choctaw Nation, Indian Territory (Present Day Oklahoma). He was born on 27 Jan 1881 in Kentuckytown, Grayson County, Texas. He died on 18 Apr 1960 in Plainview, Texas.

More About Annie Bell Bowie:
Burial: Rest Haven Cemetery, Quitaque, Texas

Notes for Annie Bell Bowie:
Listed in Choctaw Nations Marriage records (Oklahoma).

----

lived in Silverton, Texas at the time of her death.

Headstone has January 30, 1978 for date of death. Death certificate has January 31, 1978 for date of death.

More About Claude Ray Badgett:
Burial: 20 Apr 1960 in Rest Haven Cemetery, Quitaque,
Texas Cause Of Death: Heart Attack
Living In: 1900 Living with his sister, Annie and her family, in Bells, Grayson County, Texas
Living In: 1918 Bells, Texas
Occupation: 1900 in Bells, Grayson County, Texas; Drug Salesman
Occupation: 1910 in Bells, Grayson County, Texas; Druggist in his own Drug Store
Occupation: 1920 in Bells, Grayson County, Texas; Retail Drug Store Owner
Occupation: 1930 in Quitaque, Briscoe County, Texas; Retail Drug Store Merchant
Occupation: 1940 in Quitaque, Briscoe County, Texas; Pharmacist in his own Retail Drugstore

Notes for Claude Ray Badgett:
Owned his own drugstore in Bells, Texas for 28 years. Then owned a drugstore in Quitaque, Texas and later Silverton, Texas.
Lived in Silverton, Texas at the time of his death.

Claude Ray Badgett and Annie Bell Bowie had the following children:

   i. THYRA[5] BADGETT was born on 09 Feb 1903 in Indian Territory (Present Day Oklahoma). She died on 29 Oct 1967 in Houston, Texas. She married FRANK ASHBURN KING. He was born on 31 Jul 1894 in Texas. He died on 12 Apr 1977 in Dallas County, Texas.

    More About Thyra Badgett:
    Burial: 31 Oct 1967 in Oak Hill Cemetery, Whitewright,
    Texas Cause Of Death: Recurrent Cerebral Thrombosis
    Occupation: 1930 in Denison, Grayson County, Texas; Bookkeeper in Bank

15. ii. MARY BELL BADGETT was born on 19 Oct 1905 in Bells, Texas. She died on 20 Feb 1964 in Houston, Harris County, Texas. She married William Payne Savage, son of Charles Edward Savage and Flora Belle Payne on 28 Feb 1925 in Grayson County, Texas. He was born on 23 Sep 1903 in Whitewright, Texas. He died in Jul 1970 in Oklahoma City, Oklahoma.

16. iii. BARBARA ELLEN BADGETT was born on 12 Sep 1912 in Bells, Texas. She died on 03 Nov 2011 in Cockeysville, Maryland. She married Edward Eugene Younger, son of William Randolph Younger and Alma Artelia Rainbolt on 29 Jun 1936 in Quitaque, Texas. He was born on 29 Jun 1909 in Pindall, Arkansas. He died on 23 Jun 1979 in Charlottesville, Virginia.

10. **WILLIAM[4] BROWN** (Barbara Patterson[3] Bell, William[2] Bell, Joseph[1] Bell) was born on 07 Feb 1900 in Indian Territory (Present Day Oklahoma). He died on 04 Apr 1982 in Krebs, Oklahoma. He married

(UNKNOWN).

More About William Brown:
Burial: Oak Hill Memorial Park, McAlester, Oklahoma
Occupation: Coal Miner

William Brown and (Unknown) had the following child:

    i.   JACK[5] BROWN.

11.   ROBERT J.[4] MCINNIS (Elizabeth[3] Bell, William[2] Bell, Joseph[1] Bell) was born on 08 Aug 1905 in Coalgate, Oklahoma. He died on 07 Jul 1964 in Coalgate, Oklahoma. He married BILLYE PAULINE BLACK. She was born on 20 Apr 1911 in Oklahoma. She died on 12 Aug 1988.

More About Robert J. McInnis:
Burial: Coalgate Cemetery, Coalgate, Oklahoma with Rev. V. V. Voss officiating.
Living In: 1930 Robert and his wife are living with his mother in Coalgate, Oklahoma
Living In: 1940 Robert and his wife are living with his mother in Coalgate, Oklahoma
Occupation: 1930 in Coalgate, Coal County, Oklahoma; Proprietor of Confectionary
Occupation: 1940 in Coalgate, Coal County, Oklahoma; Owner and Manager of Drugstore and Cafe
Occupation: Owned and operated, with his brother C.R. McKinnis, Palace Drug Store in Coalgate, Oklahoma.
Occupation: President of Coalgate, Oklahoma Chamber of Commerce.

More About Billye Pauline Black:
Occupation: 1930 in Coalgate, Coal County, Oklahoma; Baker in Bakery
Occupation: 1940 in Coalgate, Coal County, Oklahoma; Waitress in Family Owned Cafe

Robert J. McInnis and Billye Pauline Black had the following children:

    i.   PEGGY JANE[5] MCINNIS. She married (UNKNOWN) HOLDERMAN.

    ii.   BOBBY JEAN MCINNIS.

12.   CLAUD RAY[4] MCINNIS (Elizabeth[3] Bell, William[2] Bell, Joseph[1] Bell) was born on 24 Oct 1907 in Indian Territory (Present Day Oklahoma). He died on 22 Dec 1980. He married Katherine Marie Maloney on 31 Jul 1945 in Weatherford, Texas. She was born on 17 Feb 1913 in Texas. She died on 11 Oct 1992 in Dallas, Texas.

More About Claud Ray McInnis:
Burial: Coalgate Cemetery, Coalgate, Oklahoma
Living In: 1940 Claude and his wife are living with his mother in Coalgate, Oklahoma.
Occupation: 1930 in Shawnee, Pottawatomie County, Oklahoma; Freight Line Worker
Occupation: 1940 in Coalgate, Coal County, Oklahoma; Assistant Manager in Family Owned Drug Store and Cafe

Notes for Claud Ray McInnis:
Headstone has October 24, 1906 for date of birth. Social Security death index has October 24, 1907 for date of birth.

More About Katherine Marie Maloney:
Burial: Coalgate Cemetery, Coalgate, Oklahoma
Occupation: 1940 in Coalgate, Coal County, Oklahoma; Waitress in Family Owned Cafe

Claud Ray McInnis and Katherine Marie Maloney had the following children:

      i.   Joy[5] McINNIS.

      ii.   CLAUD RAY McINNIS was born on 09 Feb 1945 in Sherman, Texas. He died on 10 May 2004 in Coalgate, Oklahoma.

          More About Claud Ray McInnis:
          Burial: Coalgate Cemetery, Coalgate, Oklahoma

      iii.   GAY McINNIS.

13.   **ALICE LOVERE[4] BELL** (James P.[3], William[2], Joseph[1]) was born on 26 Dec 1909 in Oklahoma. She died on 28 Feb 1959 in Mount Vernon, Knox County, Ohio. She married **RAYMOND L. BENTON**. He was born on 25 Feb 1905. He died on 26 May 1976 in Mount Vernon, Knox County, Ohio.

Raymond L. Benton and Alice Lovere Bell had the following child:

17.   i. LOIS LOVERE[5] BENTON was born on 10 Jan 1933 in Henryetta, Oklahoma. She died on 20 Dec 1994 in Columbus, Ohio. She married Thomas Bennett Studebaker, son of Ernest Benton Studebaker and Lucinda Bennett on 10 Apr 1959 in Mt. Vernon, Ohio. He was born on 02 Jun 1928 in Alliance, Ohio. He died on 13 Sep 1998 in Columbus, Ohio.

14.   **WILLIAM ROBERT[4] BELL** (Joseph[3], William[2], Joseph[1]) was born on 13 Jul 1922 in Coalgate, Oklahoma. He died on 04 Nov 1981 in Texas. He married Alma Louise Akerman, daughter of Donald Akerman and Theresa Diester on 11 Aug 1951 in McAllister, Oklahoma. She was born on 11 Nov 1930 in Sacred Heart, Oklahoma. She died on 22 Dec 2010 in Dallas, Texas.

More About William Robert Bell:
Burial: Saint Paul Catholic Cemetery, Saint Paul, Collin County, Texas
Living In: 1981 Wylie, Texas
Military Service: April 29, 1943 - January 19, 1946, U.S. Navy Seabee

Notes for William Robert Bell:
Served with the 90th USNCB and the 95th USNCB during World War Two. William participated in the battle for Iwo Jima with the 90th USNCB.

More About Alma Louise Akerman:
Burial: 27 Dec 2010 in Saint Paul Catholic Cemetery, Saint Paul, Collin County, Texas

William Robert Bell and Alma Louise Akerman had the following child:

18.   i. BARBARA ANN[5] BELL was born on 07 Jun 1958 in San Diego, California. She married Billy Darrell Maynard, son of Billy Edward Maynard and Karen Ann Hensley on 14 Oct 1976 in Wylie, Texas. He was born on 05 Nov 1956 in McKinney, Texas.

Generation 5

15.   **MARY BELL[5] BADGETT** (Annie Bell[4] Bowie, Barbara Patterson[3] Bell, William[2] Bell, Joseph[1] Bell) was born on 19 Oct 1905 in Bells, Texas. She died on 20 Feb 1964 in Houston, Harris County, Texas. She married William Payne Savage, son of Charles Edward Savage and Flora Belle Payne on 28 Feb 1925 in Grayson County, Texas. He was born on 23 Sep 1903 in Whitewright, Texas. He died in Jul 1970 in Oklahoma City, Oklahoma.

More About Mary Bell Badgett:
Burial: 25 Feb 1964 in Rest Haven Cemetery, Quitaque, Texas
Cause Of Death: Carcinoma of the Tongue.
Occupation: Worked for Department of State in Washington D, C.

Notes for Mary Bell Badgett:
Head stone has October 19, 1905 as birth date. Headstone has January 20, 1964 for death date
which is not correct. Death certificate has October 19, 1904 as birth date and February 20, 1964
as death date.
Born Mary Bell Badgett but known as Maribel for most of her life. Her headstone has Maribel on it.

More About William Payne Savage:
Occupation: 1930 in Amarillo, Texas; Bookkeeper in Wholesale Hardware
Occupation: 1940 in Oklahoma City, Oklahoma; Traveling Salesman for Wholesale
Hardware
Occupation: Salesman
Military Service: World War Two - U.S. Army (Captain)

Notes for William Payne Savage:
Found dead in his hotel room in Oklahoma City, Oklahoma. Exact date of death is not certain.

William Payne Savage and Mary Bell Badgett had the following children:

19. i. MARIBEL[6] SAVAGE was born on 22 Jun 1926 in Sherman Texas. She died on 14 Feb 2010
in Tampa, Florida. She married ROY GARLAND EDWARDS. He was born on 30 May 1922
in Loraine, Texas. He died on 14 Oct 1974 in Tampa, Florida.

 ii. CLAUDE RAY SAVAGE was born on 02 Jul 1933 in Briscoe County, Texas. He died
on 17 Apr 1984 in Tarrant County, Texas.

More About Claude Ray Savage:
Burial: Moore Memorial Gardens, Arlington, Texas
Living In: 1940 Living with his Badgett grandparents in Quitaque, Briscoe County,
Texas.
Military Service: U. S. Army

16. **BARBARA ELLEN**[5] **BADGETT** (Annie Bell[4] Bowie, Barbara Patterson[3] Bell, William[2] Bell,
Joseph[1] Bell) was born on 12 Sep 1912 in Bells, Texas. She died on 03 Nov 2011 in
Cockeysville, Maryland. She married Edward Eugene Younger, son of William Randolph
Younger and Alma Artelia Rainbolt on 29 Jun 1936 in Quitaque, Texas. He was born on 29
Jun 1909 in Pindall, Arkansas. He died on 23 Jun 1979 in Charlottesville, Virginia.

More About Barbara Ellen Badgett:
Burial: 13 Jul 2013 in University of Virginia Cemetery, Charlottesville,
Virginia
Living In: 05 Apr 1930 With her parents in Quitique, Texas
Living In: 23 Apr 1930 As a lodger in Oklahoma City, Oklahoma
Occupation: 1940 in Washington, D.C.; Steno-Typist

Notes for Barbara Ellen Badgett:
Barbara Badgett Younger

Barbara Badgett Younger, 99, of Charlottesville, died on Thursday, November 3, 2011,
at Broadmead in Cockeysville, Maryland.

She was born on September 11, 1912, in Bells, Texas. She was preceded in death by her husband of 49 years, Mr. Edward Younger, professor of history at the University of Virginia.

She attended schools in Bells, Texas, and El Reno, Oklahoma, and was president of her freshman class and vice-president of her sophomore class. After her junior year, she entered Oklahoma City University in 1929, where she was a member of Beta Alpha Phi sorority. She then attended West Texas State Teacher's College in Canyon, Texas, receiving a teaching certificate. As a young woman she was well known for her talent and beauty, and she was crowned Queen of the Red River Valley Fair in Paris, Texas and Queen of the "Court of America Beyond the Horizon" at the Plainview, Texas, Dairy Pageant. She began her teaching career on West Texas ranch schools, in one-room schoolhouses where the students rode to school on horseback. In 1936, she married Edward Younger, also a teacher, and 1933 graduate of Arkansas State Teachers College. Mr. Younger then began graduate study at Oklahoma State University and Mrs. Younger worked as office assistant to University president Henry G. Bennett, who was later appointed by President Truman as an Assistant Secretary of State, heading up the Point Four Program that later became USAID. The couple then moved to Washington, D.C., where Mr. Younger completed his Ph.D. in History in 1942.

There Mrs. Younger was a secretary to the Commissioner of the United States Office of Civilian Defense until she "retired" to help her husband with research and type his dissertation. During World War II, Mr. Younger joined the United States Navy and the couple lived in Florida, California, Rhode Island and finally Annapolis, Maryland. In 1946, Mr. Younger joined the faculty of the University of Virginia. He became chair of the History Department in 1962 and was appointed Dean of the Graduate School of Arts and Sciences in 1966. From 1955 until 1979, Barbara and Ed lived on the Grounds; from 1955 until 1967 at 4 Dawson's Row, and from 1967 until 1979 in Pavilion X. From 1957 until 1958, they travelled to live in India where Mr. Younger was Fulbright professor of American history at the University of Allahabad. From 1960 until 1961, they lived in Newport, RI, where Mr. Younger taught maritime history at the Naval War College. Barbara was his partner in all his endeavors for some forty years, opening her home to gatherings of students, faculty, and visiting scholars. She was active in community and University affairs: American Association of University Women, Westminster Presbyterian Church, Faculty Wives Club, where she was President from 1956 until 1957.

After the death of Mr. Younger in 1979, she helped to supervise the completion and publishing of his final book,"The Governors of Virginia Since 1860". She continued to live in Charlottesville and enjoyed an active life of entertaining and international travel until 2005, when she moved to Maryland to live nearer her family. She especially enjoyed time spent with her grandson.

Surviving are Ellen Stromdahl, daughter, Mark Stromdahl, son-in-law, and Larson Stromdahl, grandson.

A private memorial service will be held at Broadmead Retirement Community in Cockeysville, Maryland, on Thursday, November 17, 2011. Interment will be held at the University of Virginia Cemetery at a later date.

Memorial contributions can be made to the Edward and Barbara Younger Award, Corcoran Department of History, University of Virginia. Pay to the order of the College Foundation, P.O. Box 400801, Charlottesville, Virginia, 22904

Published in the Daily Progress on November 10, 2011

YOUNGER, Barbara, 99, of Charlottesville, died November 3, 2011. She was preceded in death by her husband of 49 years, Edward Younger, professor of history, University of Virginia. She received her teaching certificate at West Texas State Teacher's College and married Mr. Younger in 1936. In 1946, Mr. Younger joined the faculty of the University of Virginia, where he became chair of the History Department in 1962 and was appointed Dean of the Graduate School of Arts and Sciences in 1966. From 1955-1979, the couple lived on the University of Virginia Grounds. In 1957-58, they traveled to live in India, where Mr. Younger was Fulbright professor of University of Allahabad. In 1960-61, they lived in Newport, R.I., where Mr. Younger taught at the Naval War College. Mrs. Younger was his partner in all his endeavors for some 40 years, opening her home to gatherings of students, faculty, and visiting scholars. She was active in community and University affairs. After Mr. Younger's death in 1979, she helped to supervise the completion of his final book, "The Governors of Virginia, 1860 to 1978." She continued to live in Charlottesville until 2005, when she moved to Maryland. Surviving are Ellen Stromdahl, daughter; Mark Stromdahl, son in law; and Larson Stromdahl; grandson. A private memorial service will be held at Broadmead Retirement Community, Cockeysville, Md. on November 17. Interment will be in the University of Virginia Cemetery at a later date. Memorial contributions can be made to the Edward and Barbara Younger Award, Corcoran Department of History, University of Virginia.

Published in Richmond Times-Dispatch on November 10, 2011

Barbara Badgett Younger of Charlottesville passed away on 3 Nov. 2011, at the Broadmead Retirement Community in Cockeysville, MD, and a private memorial service of her life was held there. On Saturday, 13 July, 2013, her remains will be returned to Charlottesville and interred in the University of Virginia Cemetery.

She was born on September 11, 1912, in Bells, Texas. She was preceded in death by her husband of 49 years, Mr. Edward Younger, professor of history at the University of Virginia. She attended schools in Bells, Texas, and El Reno, Oklahoma, and was president of her freshman class and vice-president of her sophomore class. After her junior year, she entered Oklahoma City University in 1929, where she was a member of Beta Alpha Phi sorority. She then attended West Texas State Teacher's College in Canyon, Texas, receiving a teaching certificate. As a young woman she was well known for her talent and beauty, and she was crowned Queen of the Red River Valley Fair in Paris, Texas and Queen of the "Court of America Beyond the Horizon" at the Plainview, Texas, Dairy Pageant. She began her teaching career on West Texas ranch schools, in one-room schoolhouses where the students rode to school on horseback. In 1936, she married Edward Younger, also a teacher, and 1933 graduate of Arkansas State Teachers College. Mr. Younger then began graduate study at Oklahoma State University and Mrs. Younger worked as office assistant to University president Henry G. Bennett, who was later appointed by President Truman as an Assistant Secretary of State, heading up the Point Four Program that later became USAID. The couple then moved to Washington, D.C., where Mr. Younger completed his Ph.D. in History in 1942.

There Mrs. Younger was a secretary to the Commissioner of the United States Office of Civilian Defense until she "retired" to help her husband with research and type his dissertation. During World War II, Mr. Younger joined the United States Navy and the couple lived in Florida, California, Rhode Island and finally Annapolis, Maryland. In 1946, Mr. Younger joined the faculty of the University of Virginia. He became chair of the History Department in 1962 and was appointed Dean of the Graduate School of Arts and Sciences in 1966. From 1955 until 1979, Barbara and Ed lived on the Grounds; from 1955 until 1967 at 4 Dawson's Row, and from 1967 until 1979 in Pavilion X. From 1957 until 1958, they travelled to live in India where Mr. Younger was Fulbright professor of American history at the University of Allahabad. From 1960 until 1961, they lived in Newport, RI, where Mr. Younger taught maritime history at the Naval War College. Barbara was his partner in all his endeavors for some forty years, opening her home to gatherings of students, faculty, and visiting scholars. She was active in community and University affairs: American Association of University Women, Westminster Presbyterian Church, Faculty Wives Club, where she was President from 1956 until 1957.

After the death of Mr. Younger in 1979, she helped to supervise the completion and publishing of his final book, "The Governors of Virginia, 1860-1978". She continued to live in Charlottesville and enjoyed an active life of entertaining and international travel until 2005, when she moved to Maryland to live nearer her family. She especially enjoyed time spent with her grandson.

Surviving are Ellen Stromdahl, daughter, Mark Stromdahl, son-in-law, and Larson Stromdahl, grandson.

A graveside service will be held at the University of Virginia Cemetery at 11:00 am, Saturday, 13

July, 2013.

Teague Funeral Services, Charlottesville, Virginia

More About Edward Eugene Younger:
Burial: University of Virginia Cemetery, Charlottesville, Virginia
Living In: Bet. 1910-1930 Prairie Township, Searcy County, Arkansas
Living In: 17 Apr 1930 With his parents in Prarie Township. Searcy County, Arkansas.
Living In: 23 Apr 1930 As a boarder while he was a school student in Cypress Ridge, Monroe County, Arkansas.
Living In: 1940 Washington, District of Columbia
Occupation: Bet. 1928-1937; Teacher, Principal and Superintendant in Public Schools of Arkansas and Oklahoma
Occupation: Bet. 1937-1938 ; Teaching Fellow at Oklahoma State University
Occupation: Bet. 1938-1942 ; Teaching Fellow at George Washington University
Occupation: Bet. 1945-1946 ; Instructor of History, U. S. Naval Academy
Occupation: Bet. 1946-1961 ; Professor of American History, University of Virginia
Military Service: Bet. 17 Aug 1942-May 1954; U.S. Navy, World War 2 (Lt. Commander)

Notes for Edward Eugene Younger:
Head of History Department at the University of Virginia, Charlottesville, Virginia.

Edward Eugene Younger and Barbara Ellen Badgett had the following child:

20.   i. ELLEN BADGETT[6] YOUNGER was born on 05 Sep 1947 in Charlottesville, Virginia. She married (1) JAMES OTIS MOORE, son of James O. Moore on 11 Jan 1966. He was born about 1945. She married MARK STROMDAHL.

17.   LOIS LOVERE[5] BENTON (Alice Lovere[4] Bell, James P.[3] Bell, William[2] Bell, Joseph[1] Bell) was born on 10 Jan 1933 in Henryetta, Oklahoma. She died on 20 Dec 1994 in Columbus, Ohio. She married Thomas Bennett Studebaker, son of Ernest Benton Studebaker and Lucinda Bennett on 10 Apr 1959 in Mt. Vernon, Ohio. He was born on 02 Jun 1928 in Alliance, Ohio. He died on 13 Sep 1998 in Columbus, Ohio.

More About Lois Lovere Benton:
Occupation: Elementary School Teacher

More About Thomas Bennett Studebaker:
Burial: Riverview Cemetery, East Liverpool, Columbiana County, Ohio
Military Service: U.S. Army

Notes for Thomas Bennett Studebaker:
Ohio death index gives date of death as September 13, 1998. Headstone gives date of death as September 14, 1998.

Thomas Bennett Studebaker and Lois Lovere Benton had the following child:

i.   LUCINDA BENTON[6] STUDEBAKER was born on 15 Jun 1966 in Columbus, Ohio.

18.   BARBARA ANN[5] BELL (William Robert[4], Joseph[3], William[2], Joseph[1]) was born on 07 Jun 1958 in San Diego, California. She married Billy Darrell Maynard, son of Billy Edward Maynard and Karen Ann Hensley on 14 Oct 1976 in Wylie, Texas. He was born on 05 Nov 1956 in McKinney, Texas.

More About Billy Darrell Maynard:

Occupation: ; Machinist

Billy Darrell Maynard and Barbara Ann Bell had the following children:

21.   i. BRYAN JUSTIN[6] MAYNARD was born on 09 Apr 1983 in Quitman, Texas. He married Sarah Marie Hickey, daughter of Dan Patrick Hickey and Tracey Ann Blakely on 05 Aug 2005 in Havelock, North Carolina. She was born on 17 Mar 1984 in Kansas City, Missouri.

22.   ii. BRANDON MAYNARD was born on 01 Jan 1988 in Garland, Texas. He married Jessica Raye Penney, daughter of Dean Penney and Billye Turnbow Stark on 10 Nov 2012 in Farmersville, Texas. She was born on 18 Oct 1987.

Generation 6

19. **MARIBEL[6] SAVAGE** (Mary Bell[5] Badgett, Annie Bell[4] Bowie, Barbara Patterson[3] Bell, William[2] Bell, Joseph[1] Bell) was born on 22 Jun 1926 in Sherman Texas. She died on 14 Feb 2010 in Tampa, Florida. She married **ROY GARLAND EDWARDS**. He was born on 30 May 1922 in Loraine, Texas. He died on 14 Oct 1974 in Tampa, Florida.

More About Maribel Savage:
Burial: 18 Feb 2010 in Pleasant Grove Cemetery, Durant, Florida
Living In: 1940 Living with her Badgett grandparents in Quitaque, Briscoe County, Texas.

Notes for Maribel Savage:
Born Mary Bell Savage but known as Maribel most of her life. Original birth certificate does not have a first name and amended birth certificate, filed June 20, 1952, has Maribel for her first name. 1940 U.S. Census has her name as Mary Bell Savage.

More About Roy Garland Edwards:
Burial: Pleasant Grove Cemetery, Durant, Florida
Military Service: Bet. 1942-1964; U. S. Air Force (retired as a Major)

Roy Garland Edwards and Maribel Savage had the following children:

23.   i. DAVID GARLAND[7] EDWARDS was born on 21 May 1945 in Fort Sumner, New Mexico. He married Hope Ellen Stewart on 09 Mar 1968 in Tampa, Florida. She was born on 27 Jun 1949 in South Perry, Ohio.

    ii. ROBERT MARION EDWARDS was born on 11 Dec 1946 in Lubbock, Texas. Died: February 13, 2010 in San Francisco, California

20. **ELLEN BADGETT[6] YOUNGER** (Barbara Ellen[5] Badgett, Annie Bell[4] Bowie, Barbara Patterson[3] Bell, William[2] Bell, Joseph[1] Bell) was born on 05 Sep 1947 in Charlottesville, Virginia. She married (1) **JAMES OTIS MOORE**, son of James O. Moore on 11 Jan 1966. He was born about 1945. She married **MARK STROMDAHL**.

Mark Stromdahl and Ellen Badgett Younger had the following child:

    i. LARSON[7] STROMDAHL.

21. **BRYAN JUSTIN[6] MAYNARD** (Barbara Ann[5] Bell, William Robert[4] Bell, Joseph[3] Bell, William[2] Bell, Joseph[1] Bell) was born on 09 Apr 1983 in Quitman, Texas. He married Sarah Marie Hickey, daughter of Dan Patrick Hickey and Tracey Ann Blakely on 05 Aug 2005 in Havelock, North Carolina. She was born on 17 Mar 1984 in Kansas City, Missouri.

More About Bryan Justin Maynard:

Military Service: U. S. Marines

Bryan Justin Maynard and Sarah Marie Hickey had the following children:
-   i.   WILLIAM PATRICK[7] MAYNARD was born on 27 Aug 2007 in New Bern, North Carolina.

-   ii.   EMMA JUNE MAYNARD was born on 04 Jul 2008 in Portsmouth, Virginia. She died on 04 Jul 2008 in Portsmouth, Virginia.

    More About Emma June Maynard:
    Burial: 23 Jul 2008 in Saint Paul Cemetery, Saint Paul, Texas

22.   **BRANDON[6] MAYNARD** (Barbara Ann[5] Bell, William Robert[4] Bell, Joseph[3] Bell, William[2] Bell, Joseph[1] Bell) was born on 01 Jan 1988 in Garland, Texas. He married Jessica Raye Penney, daughter of Dean Penney and Billye Turnbow Stark on 10 Nov 2012 in Farmersville, Texas. She was born on 18 Oct 1987.

Brandon Maynard and Jessica Raye Penney had the following child:
-   i.   CONNER[7] MAYNARD was born on 22 Jul 2014 in Allen, Collin County, Texas.

Generation 7

23.   **DAVID GARLAND[7] EDWARDS** (Maribel[6] Savage, Mary Bell[5] Badgett, Annie Bell[4] Bowie, Barbara Patterson[3] Bell, William[2] Bell, Joseph[1] Bell) was born on 21 May 1945 in Fort Sumner, New Mexico. He married Hope Ellen Stewart on 09 Mar 1968 in Tampa, Florida. She was born on 27 Jun 1949 in South Perry, Ohio.

More About David Garland Edwards:
Military Service: Bet. Nov 1965-Nov 1967; U. S. Army

David Garland Edwards and Hope Ellen Stewart had the following children:
24.   i. DIANA GAIL[8] EDWARDS was born on 28 Mar 1969 in Plant City, Florida. She married Mark Gregory Simmons on 23 Dec 1988 in Plant City, Florida.

25.   ii. DARLENE MARIE EDWARDS was born on 28 Dec 1970 in Plant City, Florida. She married Randall Edward Thompson on 12 Sep 1993 in Pickerington, Ohio.

-   iii.   PATRICIA ANNE EDWARDS was born on 20 Oct 1972 in Plant City, Florida. She died on 20 Oct 1972 in Plant City, Florida.

Generation 8

24.   **DIANA GAIL[8] EDWARDS** (David Garland[7], Maribel[6] Savage, Mary Bell[5] Badgett, Annie Bell[4] Bowie, Barbara Patterson[3] Bell, William[2] Bell, Joseph[1] Bell) was born on 28 Mar 1969 in Plant City, Florida. She married Mark Gregory Simmons on 23 Dec 1988 in Plant City, Florida.

Mark Gregory Simmons and Diana Gail Edwards had the following children:
-   i.   MARK GREGORY[9] EDWARDS was born on 20 Jun 1988 in Plant City, Florida. He married Julie Ann Mercer on 17 Feb 2007 in Wellston, Ohio. She was born on 28 May 1988.

27.   ii. DAVIAN GAIL SIMMONS was born on 12 Feb 1991 in Monroe, North Carolina. She married JERROD ROGERS.

25. **DARLENE MARIE**[8] **EDWARDS** (David Garland[7], Maribel[6] Savage, Mary Bell[5] Badgett, Annie Bell[4] Bowie, Barbara Patterson[3] Bell, William[2] Bell, Joseph[1] Bell) was born on 28 Dec 1970 in Plant City, Florida. She married Randall Edward Thompson on 12 Sep 1993 in Pickerington, Ohio.

Randall Edward Thompson and Darlene Marie Edwards had the following children:

    i.   TREVOR[9] THOMPSON was born on 11 Sep 1995.

    ii.   VICTORIA KATHLEEN THOMPSON was born in May 1997.

Generation 9

26. **DAVIAN GAIL**[9] **SIMMONS** (Diana Gail[8] Edwards, David Garland[7] Edwards, Maribel[6] Savage, Mary Bell[5] Badgett, Annie Bell[4] Bowie, Barbara Patterson[3] Bell, William[2] Bell, Joseph[1] Bell) was born on 12 Feb 1991 in Monroe, North Carolina. She married **JERROD RODGERS**.

Jerrod Rodgers and Davian Gail Simmons had the following child:

    i.   DAVID[10] ROGERS.
    li   Cloe   Rogers

NOTES:

Descendants of Robert Patterson

Generation 1

1. **ROBERT**[1] **PATTERSON** was born about Jun 1807 in Rutherglen, Lanarkshire, Scotland. He died on 15 Mar 1873 in Silverbanks, Cambuslang, Lanarkshire, Scotland. He married **BARBARA SPEIRS**. She was born about 1814 in Tobcross, Lanarkshire, Scotland. She died on 04 Nov 1884 in Rutherglen, Lanarkshire, Scotland.

More About Robert Patterson:
Living In: 1861 Silverbanks, Cambuslang, Lanarkshire, Scotland
Living In: 02 Apr 1871 Silverbanks, Cambuslang, Lanarkshire, Scotland
Occupation: 1861 in Cambuslang, Lanarkshire, Scotland; Coal Miner
Occupation: 02 Apr 1871 in Cambuslang, Lanarkshire, Scotland; Coal Miner

Notes for Robert Patterson:
Death record says he was 65 and 9/12 years old at the time of his
death. Parents names are on his death record.

Notes for Barbara Speirs:
Death record says she was 70 years old at the time of her death.

Robert Patterson and Barbara Speirs had the following children:

    i.   ROBERT[2] PATTERSON was born on 17 Mar 1835 in Cambuslang, Lanark, Scotland.

    ii.   AGNES NAISMITH PATTERSON was born on 28 Feb 1837 in Cambuslang, Lanarkshire, Scotland.

    iii.   MARGARET MCALPINE PATTERSON was born on 02 Aug 1839 in Rutherglen, Lanarkshire, Scotland.

    iv.   ARCHIBALD SPEIRS PATTERSON was born on 17 Sep 1841 in Rutherglen, Lanarkshire, Scotland.

    v.   BARBARA PATTERSON was born on 19 Jul 1843 in Rutherglen, Lanarkshire, Scotland.

2.   vi. ANN KIRKWOOD PATTERSON was born on 15 May 1846 in Silverbanks,Cambuslang, Lanarkshire, Scotland. She died on 07 Jan 1934 in Coalgate, Oklahoma. She married William Bell, son of Joseph Bell and Elizabeth McLachlan on 01 Jan 1866 in Carnbuslang, Lanarkshire, Scotland. He was born on 16 May 1845 in Glasgow, Lanarkshire, Scotland. He died on 18 Mar 1924 in Coalgate, Oklahoma.

    vii.   JAMES SPEIRS PATTERSON was born on 19 Jul 1848 in Cambuslang, Lanarkshire, Scotland.

3.   viii. GILBERT PATTERSON was born on 18 May 1851 in Rutherglen, Lanarkshire, Scotland. He died between 12 Jun 1900-25 Apr 1910. He married Ann Patterson, daughter of Charles Patterson and Janet Neil on 01 Jan 1873 in Silverbanks, Cambuslang, Lanark, Scotland. She was born in Aug 1847 in Scotland. She died after 25 Apr 1910.

    ix.   ELIZABETH PATTERSON was born on 15 Jun 1854 in Rutherglen, Lanarkshire, Scotland.

4.   x. WILLIAM KIRKWOOD PATTERSON was born on 14 Apr 1858 in Rutherglen, Lanarkshire,
            Scotland. He died on 30 Aug 1937 in Detroit, Michigan. He married Elizabeth
            Duncan on 06 Feb 1882 in McAlester, Indian Territory (Present Day Oklahoma).
            She was born in Oct 1859 in Rutherglen, Lanarkshire, Scotland. She died on 20 Jul
            1943 in Pleasant Valley (near Schulter), Oklahoma.

Generation 2

2. **ANN KIRKWOOD**[2] **PATTERSON** (Robert[1]) was born on 15 May 1846 in Silverbanks,Cambuslang,
    Lanarkshire, Scotland. She died on 07 Jan 1934 in Coalgate, Oklahoma. She married William
    Bell, son of Joseph Bell and Elizabeth McLachlan on 01 Jan 1866 in Carnbuslang, Lanarkshire,
    Scotland. He was born on 16 May 1845 in Glasgow, Lanarkshire, Scotland. He died on 18 Mar
    1924 in Coalgate, Oklahoma.

More About Ann Kirkwood Patterson:
Burial: 09 Jan 1934 in Coalgate Cemetery, Coalgate, Oklahoma
Immigration: 22 Jul 1871 Arrived in New York, New York on ship "India"
Living In: 02 Apr 1871 Ann and her children are living with her parents in Silverbanks,
Cambuslang, Lanarkshire, Scotland.
Living In: Jun 1880 Delta, Keokuk County, Iowa
Living In: 1930 Coalgate, Coal County, Oklahoma

Notes for Ann Kirkwood Patterson: Headstone
has May 16, 1846 for date of birth.

More About William Bell:
Burial: 20 Mar 1924 in Coalgate Cemetery, Coalgate, Oklahoma
Immigration: Mar 1869 in From Scotland to Maryland
Occupation: 1866 in Cambuslang, Lanarkshire, Scotland; Coal Miner
Occupation: 07 Jul 1870 in Election District number 16, Allegany County, Maryland;
Miner
Occupation: 1879 in Krebs, Indian Territory (Present Day Oklahoma); Coal Miner
Occupation: 1900 in Coalgate, Choctaw Nation, Indian Territory (Present Day Oklahoma);
Coal Miner
Occupation: 1910 in Coalgate, Oklahoma; Retired
Occupation: 1920 in Coalgate, Oklahoma; Retired

William Bell and Ann Kirkwood Patterson had the following children:

5.   i. BARBARA PATTERSON[3] BELL was born on 03 Mar 1867 in Silverbanks, Cambuslang,
            Lanarkshire, Scotland. She died on 12 Mar 1936 in Oklahoma City, Oklahoma. She
            married ALEXANDER BOWIE. He was born about 22 Dec 1858 in Pennsylvania. He died
            on 04 Mar 1889 in McAlester, Indian Territory (Present Day Oklahoma). She married
            (2) ROBERT H. BROWN on 13 Sep 1893 in Thurber, Erath County, Texas. He was born
            on 08 May 1867 in Scotland. He died on 25 Dec 1950 in St Louis, Missouri.

        ii. JOSEPH BELL was born on 22 Mar 1869 in Dalserf, Lanarkshire, Scotland. He
            died on 08 May 1882 in Indian Territory (Present Day Oklahoma).

            More About Joseph Bell:
            Burial: McAlester Cemetery, McAlester, Oklahoma

6.   iii. WILLIAM BELL was born in 1872 in Maryland. He died in 1954 in Illinois. He married
            (1) MARGARET KERR, daughter of Thomas Kerr about 1893. She was born on 08 Jul
            1873 in Scotland. She died on 17 Mar 1921 in Collinsville, Illinois. He married (2)

ROSE KAUFMAN about 1923. She was born on 30 Aug 1890 in Carlinville,
Illinois. She died in Jan 1980 in Alton, Madison County, Illinois.

iv.   ROBERT H. BELL was born on 08 Sep 1874 in Maryland. He died on 07 Nov 1902.
He married Mary M. Boozle on 16 May 1897 in Muscogee County, Indian
Territory, (present day Oklahoma).

More About Robert H. Bell:
Burial: Coalgate Cemetery, Coalgate, Oklahoma
Occupation: 1900 in Madrid, Santa Fe County, New Mexico; Coal Miner

Notes for Robert H. Bell:
1900 U.S. census shows Robert was married about 1897 and still married in
1900. He was living as a boarder in 1900.

7.   v. ELIZABETH BELL was born in Aug 1879 in Iowa. She died on 11 Aug 1960 in Coalgate,
Oklahoma. She married John McInnis, son of John McInnes and Mary Belle
VanBrocklin in Feb 1902 in Coalgate, Choctaw Nation, Indian Territory (Present Day
Oklahoma). He was born on 15 Dec 1878 in Ohio. He died on 20 Aug 1918 in
Coalgate, Oklahoma.

8.   vi. JAMES P. BELL was born on 17 Dec 1880 in Iowa. He died in Aug 1966 in Oklahoma.
He married Isabel Liddle on 05 Jun 1909 in Coalgate, Coal County, Oklahoma. She
was born about 1886 in Indian Territory (Present Day Oklahoma).

9.   vii. JOSEPH BELL was born on 13 Jun 1883 in Krebs, Indian Territory (Present Day
Oklahoma). He died on 27 Oct 1958 in Coalgate, Oklahoma. He married Emily Louise
Connally, daughter of Charles Clay Connaly and Willie Etta Jenkins on 18 Nov 1906
in Choctaw Nation, Indian Territory (Present Day Oklahoma). She was born on 10
Aug 1885 in Huntsville, Alabama. She died on 07 Oct 1951 in Coalgate, Oklahoma.

10.   viii. GEORGE PATTERSON BELL was born on 07 May 1886 in Krebs, Indian Territory
(Oklahoma). He died on 04 Sep 1949 in Gorman, Texas. He married Blanche Lee
Hanlin on 26 Feb 1907 in Coalgate, Choctaw Nation, Indian Territory (Present Day
Oklahoma). She was born on 06 Mar 1887 in Mississippi. She died on 27 Jan 1963 in
Oklahoma.

3.   **GILBERT**^{2} **PATTERSON** (Robert^1) was born on 18 May 1851 in Rutherglen, Lanarkshire, Scotland.
He died between 12 Jun 1900-25 Apr 1910. He married Ann Patterson, daughter of Charles
Patterson and Janet Neil on 01 Jan 1873 in Silverbanks, Cambuslang, Lanark, Scotland. She
was born in Aug 1847 in Scotland. She died after 25 Apr 1910.

More About Gilbert Patterson:
Emigration: 01 Feb 1882 in New York, New York
Occupation: 1873 in Cambuslang, Lanark, Scotland; Coal Miner
Occupation: 1900 in Township 5, Choctaw Nation, Indian Territory (present day Oklahoma);
Coal Miner

Notes for Gilbert Patterson:
Arrived in New York, New York February 1, 1882 on SS Italy.

Transcription of birth record in Scotland gives first name as Gabriel.

More About Ann Patterson:
Emigration: 1888
Living In: 1910 Krebs Ward 3, Pittsburg County, Oklahoma
Occupation: 1873 in Cambuslang, Lanark, Scotland; Paper Mill Worker

Gilbert Patterson and Ann Patterson had the following children:

i. ROBERT[3] PATTERSON was born about 1874 in Scotland.

ii. CHARLES PATTERSON was born in May 1875 in Scotland.

> More About Charles Patterson:
> Immigration: 1888
> Living In: 1910 With his mother in Krebs Ward 3, Pittsburg County, Oklahoma.
> Occupation: 1910 in Krebs Ward 3, Pittsburg County, Oklahoma; Coal Miner

iii. ANN PATTERSON was born in Feb 1881 in Scotland. She died on 30 Jul 1925. She married RALPH CROWDER. He was born in 1877 in Illinois. He died in 1948.

> More About Ann Patterson:
> Burial: Oak Hill Memorial Park, McAlester, Pittsburg County, Oklahoma
> Immigration: 1888

iv. JEANETTE PATTERSON was born on 26 Dec 1884 in Scotland. She died in Mar 1967 in Oklahoma.

> More About Jeanette Patterson:
> Burial: Oak Hill Memorial Park, McAlester, Pittsburg County, Oklahoma
> Immigration: 1888
> Living In: 1910 With her mother in Krebs Ward 3, Pittsburg County, Oklahoma.

v. GILBERT PATTERSON was born on 01 Dec 1888. He died on 18 Apr 1892.

> More About Gilbert Patterson:
> Burial: North McAlester Cemetery, McAlester, Oklahoma

iv. **WILLIAM KIRKWOOD[2] PATTERSON** (Robert[1]) was born on 14 Apr 1858 in Rutherglen, Lanarkshire, Scotland. He died on 30 Aug 1937 in Detroit, Michigan. He married Elizabeth Duncan on 06 Feb 1882 in McAlester, Indian Territory (Present Day Oklahoma). She was born in Oct 1859 in Rutherglen, Lanarkshire, Scotland. She died on 20 Jul 1943 in Pleasant Valley (near Schulter), Oklahoma.

More About William Kirkwood Patterson:
Burial: 02 Sep 1937 in Westlawn Cemetery, Henryetta, Oklahoma
Occupation: 1900 in Coalgate, Choctaw Nation, Indian Territory (Present Day Oklahoma); Coal Miner
Occupation: 1910 in Murray, Coal County, Oklahoma; Coal Miner
Occupation: 1920 in Murray, Coal County, Oklahoma; Coal Miner
Occupation: 1930 in Shulter, Okmulgee County, Oklahoma; Retired

Notes for William Kirkwood Patterson:
Was visiting his daughter, Agnes, in Detroit, Michigan when he died.
1910 and 1930 U.S. census gives year of Immigration as 1881.

Patterson family Bible gives date of birth as April 14, 1858. Scotland Births and Baptisms gives date of birth as April 16, 1858.

More About Elizabeth Duncan:
Burial: 23 Jul 1943 in Westlawn Cemetery, Henryetta,
Oklahoma
Immigration: 01 Feb 1882 in New York, New York

Notes for Elizabeth Duncan:
Arrived in New York, New York February 1, 1882 on SS Italy. Escorted on voyage by Gilbert Patterson.

More About William Kirkwood Patterson and Elizabeth Duncan:
Marriage Fact: Married by Reverend Will Hicks

William Kirkwood Patterson and Elizabeth Duncan had the following children:

11.   i. ROBERT[3] PATTERSON was born on 13 Dec 1882 in McAlester, Indian Territory (Present Day Oklahoma). He married ANNIE WARD. She was born about 1885 in Illinois.

12.   ii. MARY PATTERSON was born on 18 Feb 1885 in McAlester, Indian Territory (Present Day Oklahoma). She died in 1959. She married John Henderson Hall, son of John Henderson Hall and Jane Wallace on 25 Jan 1905 in Coalgate, Coal County, Choctaw Nation, Indian Territory (present day Oklahoma). He was born on 28 Jun 1881 in Bathgate, West Lothian, Scotland. He died in Nov 1967 in Oklahoma.

         iii.   BARBRA PATTERSON was born on 29 Sep 1887 in Williamsburgh, Colorado. She died on 03 Sep 1895.

                 More About Barbra Patterson:
                 Burial: Coalgate Cemetery, Coalgate, Oklahoma

                 Notes for Barbra Patterson:
                 First name is spelled Barbra on headstone.

         iv.   ANN PATTERSON was born on 14 Nov 1889 in Coalgate, Indian Territory (Present Day Oklahoma). She married ARCHIBALD MOWAT.

         v.   JEAN PATTERSON was born on 14 Feb 1892 in Coalgate, Choctaw Nation, Indian Territory (Present Day Oklahoma). She died on 05 Sep 1974 in Henryetta, Oklahoma.

                 More About Jean Patterson:
                 Occupation: Clerical Secretary

13.   vi. AGNES PATTERSON was born on 20 Mar 1895 in Coalgate, Indian Territory (Present

Day Oklahoma). She married CHARLES SOUTH.

14.   vii. WILLIAM M. PATTERSON was born on 12 Dec 1898 in Dow, Indian Territory (Present Day Oklahoma). He married LOUISE BELICK.

15.   viii. GILBERT PATTERSON was born on 26 Oct 1901 in Coalgate, Indian Territory (Present Day Oklahoma). He died on 18 Jun 1933 in Belleview, Illinois. He married Anna Adams on 26 Sep 1921 in Schulter, Oklahoma. She was born about 1904 in Ohio.

Generation 3

5.   **BARBARA PATTERSON**[3] **BELL** (Ann Kirkwood[2] Patterson, Robert[1] Patterson) was born on 03 Mar 1867 in Silverbanks, Cambuslang, Lanarkshire, Scotland. She died on 12 Mar 1936 in Oklahoma City, Oklahoma. She married **ALEXANDER BOWIE**. He was born about 22 Dec 1858 in Pennsylvania. He died on 04 Mar 1889 in McAlester, Indian Territory (Present Day Oklahoma). She married (2) **ROBERT H. BROWN** on 13 Sep 1893 in Thurber, Erath County, Texas. He was born on 08 May 1867 in Scotland. He died on 25 Dec 1950 in St Louis, Missouri.

More About Barbara Patterson Bell:
Burial: 15 Mar 1936 in Coalgate Cemetery, Coalgate, Oklahoma
Immigration: 22 Jul 1871 in Arrived in New York, New York on ship "India"

Notes for Barbara Patterson Bell:
Headstone has February 24, 1868 for date of birth.

More About Alexander Bowie:
Burial: North McAlester Cemetery, McAlester, Oklahoma

Alexander Bowie and Barbara Patterson Bell had the following child:

    1   ANNIE BELL[4] BOWIE was born on 11 Mar 1886 in Krebs, Indian Territory (Present Day Oklahoma). She died on 31 Jan 1978 in Amarillo, Potter County, Texas. She married Claude Ray Badgett, son of James Royal Badgett and Mary Belle Wakefield on 16 Apr 1902 in Coalgate, Choctaw Nation, Indian Territory (Present Day Oklahoma). He was born on 27 Jan 1881 in Kentuckytown, Grayson County, Texas. He died on 18 Apr 1960 in Plainview, Texas.

        More About Annie Bell Bowie:
        Burial: Rest Haven Cemetery, Quitaque, Texas

        Notes for Annie Bell Bowie:
        Listed in Choctaw Nations Marriage records (Oklahoma).
        ----
        lived in Silverton, Texas at the time of her death.

        Headstone has January 30, 1978 for date of death. Death certificate has January 31, 1978 for date of death.

More About Robert H. Brown:
Burial: 29 Dec 1950 in Coalgate Cemetery, Coalgate, Oklahoma
Living In: 1935 in Oklahoma City, Oklahoma

Occupation: 1900 in Coalgate, Choctaw Nation, Indian Territory (Present Day Oklahoma);
Coal Miner
Occupation: 1910 in Coalgate, Coal County, Oklahoma; Coal Mine Fire
Boss
Occupation: 1920 in Coalgate, Coal County, Oklahoma; Miner
Occupation: 1930 in Coalgate, Coal County, Oklahoma; District Inspector of Coal
Mines
Occupation: Bet. 1931-1947; Chief Mine Inspector for Oklahoma

Notes for Robert H. Brown:
Arrived in United States from Scotland in 1881.

Robert H. Brown and Barbara Patterson Bell had the following children:

    i.   AGNES[4] BROWN was born on 25 Jun 1894 in Indian Territory (Present Day
    Oklahoma). She died in Jun 1981 in Fort Smith, Arkansas. She married S. O.
    HENSHAW.

    ii.   ELIZABETH BROWN was born in Apr 1898 in Indian Territory (Present
    Day Oklahoma).

    More About Elizabeth Brown:
    Living In: Bet. 1920-1940 in Living with her parents.
    Occupation: 1920 in Coalgate, Coal County, Oklahoma; School Teacher
    Occupation: 1930 in Coalgate, Coal County, Oklahoma; Public School Teacher
    Occupation: 1940 in Oklahoma City, Oklahoma; Deputy County Clerk

    iii.   WILLIAM BROWN was born on 07 Feb 1900 in Indian Territory (Present Day
    Oklahoma). He died on 04 Apr 1982 in Krebs, Oklahoma. He married (UNKNOWN).

    More About William Brown:
    Burial: Oak Hill Memorial Park, McAlester,
    Oklahoma
    Occupation: Coal Miner

    iv.   REGINA BROWN was born on 28 Jun 1903 in Indian Territory (Present Day Oklahoma).
    She died in Oct 1986 in Fort Smith, Arkansas. She married (UNKNOWN)
    BOOTH.

    v.   ROBERT BROWN was born about Feb 1909 in Oklahoma.

    Notes for Robert Brown:
    Robert is only seen on the 1910 U.S. census for Coalgate, Oklahoma.

6   WILLIAM[3] BELL (Ann Kirkwood[2] Patterson, Robert[1] Patterson) was born in 1872 in Maryland. He died
    in 1954 in Illinois. He married (1) **MARGARET KERR**, daughter of Thomas Kerr about 1893. She was
    born on 08 Jul 1873 in Scotland. She died on 17 Mar 1921 in Collinsville, Illinois. He married
    ii. **ROSE KAUFMAN** about 1923. She was born on 30 Aug 1890 in Carlinville, Illinois. She died
    in Jan 1980 in Alton, Madison County, Illinois.

    More About William Bell:
    Burial: Bethalto United Methodist Church Cemetery, Bethalto, Illinois
    Occupation: 1900 in Precinct 10, Las Animas County, Colorado; Coal Miner

Occupation: 1910 in Collinsville, Madison County, Illinois; Coal Miner
Occupation: 1920 in Collinsville, Madison County, Illinois; Coal Miner
Occupation: 1930 in Bethalto, Madison County, Illinois; Coal Miner

Notes for William Bell:
In 1900 William was working in Las Animas County, Colorado while Margaret was living in Cerrillos, New Mexico with their children.

More About Margaret Kerr:
Burial: 20 Mar 1921 in St. John Cemetery, Collinsville, Illinois
Living In: 1900 Cerrilos, Santa Fe County, New Mexico

Notes for Margaret Kerr:
Margaret was living, with her children, in Cerrillos, New Mexico in 1900 while William was working in Las Animas County, Colorado.

William Bell and Margaret Kerr had the following children:

i. WILLIAM[4] BELL was born on 28 Sep 1894 in Coalgate, Choctaw Nation, Indian Territory (Present Day Oklahoma).

  More About William Bell:
  Occupation: 1910 in Collinsville, Madison County, Illinois; Drug Salesman
  Occupation: 1917 in Detroit, Michigan; Street Car Conductor

ii. AGNES BELL was born on 29 Jul 1897 in Madrid, New Mexico. She died on 22 Feb 1938 in Belleville, Sr. Clair County, Illinois. She married HARRY NAY. He was born on 13 Aug 1898 in Illinois. He died in Sep 1983 in Illinois.

  More About Agnes Bell:
  Burial: 25 Feb 1938 in St. John Cemetery, Collinsville Madison County, Illinois
  Living In: 1920   Living with her parents in Collinsville, Illinois.
  Living In: 1938 Collinsville, Madison County, Illinois
  Occupation: 1920 in Collinsville, Madison County, Illinois; Clerk in Railroad Office

iii. JOHN V. BELL was born in Feb 1899 in New Mexico.

  More About John V. Bell:
  Occupation: 1920 in Collinsville, Madison County, Illinois; Clerk in Railroad Office

More About Rose Kaufman:
Burial: Bethalto United Methodist Church Cemetery, Bethalto, Illinois

7 ELIZABETH[3] BELL (Ann Kirkwood[2] Patterson, Robert[1] Patterson) was born in Aug 1879 in Iowa. She died on 11 Aug 1960 in Coalgate, Oklahoma. She married John McInnis, son of John McInnes and Mary Belle VanBrocklin in Feb 1902 in Coalgate, Choctaw Nation, Indian Territory (Present Day Oklahoma). He was born on 15 Dec 1878 in Ohio. He died on 20 Aug 1918 in Coalgate, Oklahoma.

More About Elizabeth Bell:

Burial: 14 Aug 1960 in Coalgate Cemetery, Coalgate, Oklahoma
Occupation: 1900 in Coalgate, Choctaw Nation, Indian Territory (Present Day
Oklahoma); Saleswoman in Drugstore
Occupation: 1920 in Coalgate, Coal County, Oklahoma; Saleswoman in Drugstore
Occupation: 1930 in Coalgate, Coal County, Oklahoma; Retail Dry Goods Saleswoman

Notes for Elizabeth Bell:
Elizabeth McInnis Claimed by death at Home. Services for Elizabeth McInnis were held at the
First Methodist church at 2 o'clock Sunday afternoon by Daniel Forbes, Mrs. McInnis and her
husband, John McInnis, came to Coalgate 66 years ago from Krebs, and he preceded her in
death 42 years ago, She died quietly at sleep at her home here Thursday. Mrs. McInnis worked
for many years in the Corner Drug store and Margaret Covington's ready to wear store here. She
was active in the Coalgate Garden Club. Linger Longer Embroidery Club, and the order of the
Eastern Star. Surviving are two sons, C. R, McInnis, R. M. McInnis, and a daughter, Mrs. Peggy
Helvey, one brother, Jim Bell of Henrietta, five grandchildren, and five great grandchildren. Pall
bearers were W. E. Larecy, W. H. Bailey, Eddie Cox, Arthur Pope, Jim Farrimond, and Elmo
Childers. Among the out of town relatives attending the services were Mrs. Agnes Hinshaw and
Jean Booth of Ft. Smith, Ark; Mr. and Mrs. Billy Bell and daughter, and Bobbie Jean McInnis of
Oklahoma City; Louise Sugar of Londoner, MD, Mrs. George Bell of Oklahoma City; Emma Doris
Wyche of Durant, Jean Patterson and Annie Mowatt of Oklahoma City; Bob Patterson, John Hall
and daughter of Henrietta; Mr. and Mrs. John Jones, Mrs. Ted Henderson of Wapanucha; Mrs.
Harry Miller and granddaughter, Cynthia, Mrs. Ethel Harwell of Ada; Sam Covington, Mr. & Mrs.
Bill Cowan of Oklahoma City. Burial was at Coalgate cemetery with Slater funeral home directing.

More About John McInnis:
Burial: Coalgate Cemetery, Coalgate, Oklahoma
Occupation: 1900 in Coalgate, Choctaw Nation, Indian Territory (Present Day
Oklahoma); Bookkeeper
Occupation: 1910 in Coalgate, Coal County, Oklahoma; Livery Stable Prioprietor

Notes for John McInnis:
Headstone has last name spelled McInnis.

John McInnis and Elizabeth Bell had the following children:

  i. ROBERT J.[4] MCINNIS was born on 08 Aug 1905 in Coalgate, Oklahoma. He died on 07
   Jul 1964 in Coalgate, Oklahoma. He married BILLYE PAULINE BLACK. She was born
   on 20 Apr 1911 in Oklahoma. She died on 12 Aug 1988.

   More About Robert J. McInnis:
   Burial: Coalgate Cemetery, Coalgate, Oklahoma with Rev. V. V. Voss
   officiating.
   Living In: 1930 Robert and his wife are living with his mother in Coalgate,
   Oklahoma
   Living In: 1940 Robert and his wife are living with his mother in Coalgate,
   Oklahoma
   Occupation: 1930 in Coalgate, Coal County, Oklahoma; Proprietor of
   Confectionary
   Occupation: 1940 in Coalgate, Coal County, Oklahoma; Owner and Manager of
   Drugstore and Cafe
   Occupation: Owned and operated, with his brother C.R. McKinnis, Palace Drug
   Store in Coalgate, Oklahoma.
   Occupation: President of Coalgate, Oklahoma Chamber of Commerce.

    ii.   CLAUD RAY MCINNIS was born on 24 Oct 1907 in Indian Territory (Present Day Oklahoma). He died on 22 Dec 1980. He married Katherine Marie Maloney on 31 Jul 1945 in Weatherford, Texas. She was born on 17 Feb 1913 in Texas. She died on 11 Oct 1992 in Dallas, Texas.

More About Claud Ray McInnis:
Burial: Coalgate Cemetery, Coalgate, Oklahoma
Living In: 1940 Claude and his wife are living with his mother in Coalgate, Oklahoma.
Occupation: 1930 in Shawnee, Pottawatomie County, Oklahoma; Freight Line Worker
Occupation: 1940 in Coalgate, Coal County, Oklahoma; Assistant Manager in Family Owned Drug Store and Cafe

Notes for Claud Ray McInnis:
Headstone has October 24, 1906 for date of birth. Social Security death index has October 24, 1907 for date of birth.

    iii.   ANNABELL MCINNIS was born in 1911 in Oklahoma. She married (UNKNOWN) HELVEY.

8.   **JAMES P.^{3} BELL** (Ann Kirkwood^2 Patterson, Robert^1 Patterson) was born on 17 Dec 1880 in Iowa. He died in Aug 1966 in Oklahoma. He married Isabel Liddle on 05 Jun 1909 in Coalgate, Coal County, Oklahoma. She was born about 1886 in Indian Territory (Present Day Oklahoma).

More About James P. Bell:
Living In: 1930 As a boarder in Detroit, Michigan.
Living In: 1966 Henryetta, Oklahoma
Occupation: 1900 in Coalgate, Choctaw Nation, Indian Territory (Present Day Oklahoma); Coal Miner
Occupation: 1910 in Coalgate, Oklahoma; Coal Miner
Occupation: 1918 in Henryetta, Oklahoma; Working for Blackstone Coal Mine in Henryetta, Oklahoma
Occupation: 1920 in Henryetta, Oklahoma; Coal Miner
Occupation: 1930 in Detroit, Michigan; Factory Worker
Occupation: 1940 in Henryetta, Oklahoma; Field Representative for Coal Company

Notes for James P. Bell:

World War One draft registration gives December 17, 1879 as date of birth. Social Security death index gives December 17, 1880 as date of birth. James is not on 1880 U.S. census taken June 22, 1880 in Iowa. World War Two draft registration gives date of birth as December 17, 1880.

More About Isabel Liddle:
Living In: 1930 Henryetta. Oklahoma

Notes for Isabel Liddle:
First name is Isabel on marriage certificate.

James P. Bell and Isabel Liddle had the following children:

    i.   ALICE LOVERE^4 BELL was born on 26 Dec 1909 in Oklahoma. She died on 28 Feb 1959 in Mount Vernon, Knox County, Ohio. She married RAYMOND L. BENTON. He was born on 25 Feb 1905. He died on 26 May 1976 in Mount Vernon, Knox County,

Ohio.

ii.   ANNA MAE BELL was born about 1916 in Oklahoma.

iii.   JAMES P. BELL was born on 23 May 1922 in Oklahoma. He died on 07 Jul 1953 in Mediterranean Sea.

More About James P. Bell:
Burial: 29 Sep 1953 in Arlington National
Cemetery Cause Of Death: Aircraft Crash
Military Service: ; Bet. July 1, 1943 -July 7, 1953, United States Marine Corps

Notes for James P. Bell:
Died in an aircraft crash while serving in the Marine Corps on the Mediterranean Sea. Served in World War Two and the Korean War as a fighter pilot. Rank at time of death was Major.

The President of the United States of America takes pleasure in presenting the Distinguished Flying Cross to Captain James P. Bell (MCSN: 0-29498), United States Marine Corps, for heroism while participating in aerial flight as a pilot attached to a Marine Aircraft Group from 19 September to November 1950. Captain Bell successfully completed his first through thirty-fifth combat mission in support of our ground forces, destroying and inflicting great damage to concentrations of North Korean vehicles, material and personnel. By his airmanship and devotion to duty in the face of enemy anti-aircraft fire, he contributed materially to the success of our troops. His conduct throughout was in keeping with the highest traditions of the United States Naval Service.
General Orders: Commanding General 1st Marine Aircraft Wing: Serial: 3864 (April 28, 1951)
Action Date: September 19 - November
1950 Service: Marine Corps
Rank: Captain

Citation dated

April 28, 1951

The President of the United States of America takes pleasure in presenting a Gold Star in lieu of a Second Award of the Distinguished Flying Cross to Captain James P. Bell (MCSN: 0-29498), United States Marine Corps, for extraordinary achievement while participating in aerial flight as a pilot of a fighter plane against the enemy on 6 June 1951. Captain Bell while leading a four plane flight on a close air support mission east of the Kweach'on Reservoir in Korea, worked in conjunction with a Marine Ground Controller whose progress was being held up by several hundred Chinese Communist troops. In spite of intense small arms fire and extremely adverse weather conditions, Captain Bell repeatedly led his flight in attacking entrenched enemy troops at minimum altitude with napalm, rockets and strafing. These successful attacks enabled the United Nations forces to occupy this important objective with negligible opposition. Three hundred dead enemy were confirmed by the occupying forces. With unerring judgment and outstanding airmanship, Captain Bell dealt a damaging blow to the enemy. In so doing his alertness and efficient actions were in keeping with the highest traditions of the United States Naval Service.
General Orders: Commanding General 1st Marine Aircraft Wing: Serial: 6672 (July

21, 1951)
Action Date: June 6,
1951 Service: Marine
Corps Rank: Captain

Citation dated

July 21, 1951

----

    iv.   WILLIAM DAVID BELL was born about 1925 in Oklahoma.

9.   JOSEPH³ BELL (Ann Kirkwood² Patterson, Robert¹ Patterson) was born on 13 Jun 1883 in Krebs, Indian Territory (Present Day Oklahoma). He died on 27 Oct 1958 in Coalgate, Oklahoma. He married Emily Louise Connally, daughter of Charles Clay Connaly and Willie Etta Jenkins on 18 Nov 1906 in Choctaw Nation, Indian Territory (Present Day Oklahoma). She was born on 10 Aug 1885 in Huntsville, Alabama. She died on 07 Oct 1951 in Coalgate, Oklahoma.

More About Joseph Bell:
Burial: 30 Oct 1958 in Coalgate, Oklahoma
Occupation: 1900 in Coalgate, Choctaw Nation, Indian Territory (Present Day Oklahoma); Coal Miner
Occupation: 1910 in Coalgate, Coal County, Oklahoma; Pharmacist in Drug Store
Occupation: 1920 in Coalgate, Coal County, Oklahoma; Drug Store Proprietor
Occupation: 1930 in Coalgate, Coal County, Oklahoma; Druggist in Retail Drug Store
Occupation: 1940 in Coalgate, Coal County, Oklahoma; Druggist in Drug Store

Notes for Joseph Bell:
Owned his own drugstore in Coalgate, Oklahoma.
Funeral Record gives birth date as June 13, 1882. Headstone gives year of birth as 1882.
World War One and World War Two draft registrations give date of birth as June 13, 1883.
Marriage record indicates birth year of 1883.

More About Emily Louise Connally:
Burial: 09 Oct 1951 in Coalgate Cemetery, Coalgate, Oklahoma, Rev. Frank Warnke officiating
Occupation: 1940 in Coalgate, Coal County, Oklahoma; Assistant in Drug Store

Joseph Bell and Emily Louise Connally had the following children:
    i.   LOUISE H.⁴ BELL was born on 01 Dec 1907 in Oklahoma. She died on 18 Dec 1988 in Kaufman County, Texas. She married LEE SHUGAR. He was born about 1905. She married (2) LEO K. HUGHES on 26 Jan 1929 in Durant, Bryan County, Oklahoma. He was born about 1905.

    More About Louise H. Bell:
    Burial: Saint Paul Cemetery, Saint Paul, Texas

    ii.   JOSEPH CONNALLY BELL was born on 26 Oct 1910 in Coalgate, Oklahoma. He died on 21 Sep 1979 in Las Vegas, Nevada.

    More About Joseph Connally Bell:
    Burial: Woodlawn Cemetery, Las Vegas, Nevada

Military Service: Enlisted in U.S. Army at Los Angeles, California on November 20, 1943

iii. WILLIAM ROBERT BELL was born on 13 Jul 1922 in Coalgate, Oklahoma. He died on 04 Nov 1981 in Texas. He married Alma Louise Akerman, daughter of Donald Akerman and Theresa Diester on 11 Aug 1951 in McAllister, Oklahoma. She was born on 11 Nov 1930 in Sacred Heart, Oklahoma. She died on 22 Dec 2010 in Dallas, Texas.

More About William Robert Bell:
Burial: Saint Paul Catholic Cemetery, Saint Paul, Collin County, Texas
Living In: 1981 Wylie, Texas
Military Service: April 29, 1943 - January 19, 1946, U.S. Navy Seabee

Notes for William Robert Bell:
Served with the 90th USNCB and the 95th USNCB during World War Two. William participated in the battle for Iwo Jima with the 90th USNCB.

10. **GEORGE PATTERSON**[3] **BELL** (Ann Kirkwood[2] Patterson, Robert[1] Patterson) was born on 07 May 1886 in Krebs, Indian Territory (Oklahoma). He died on 04 Sep 1949 in Gorman, Texas. He married Blanche Lee Hanlin on 26 Feb 1907 in Coalgate, Choctaw Nation, Indian Territory (Present Day Oklahoma). She was born on 06 Mar 1887 in Mississippi. She died on 27 Jan 1963 in Oklahoma.

More About George Patterson Bell:
Burial: 06 Sep 1949 in Coalgate Cemetery, Coalgate, Oklahoma
Living In: 1940 George and Blanche are living with their son in law and daughter in Hugo, Oklahoma.
Occupation: 1910 in Hobart, Kiowa County, Oklahoma; Sewing Machine Agent
Occupation: 1916 in Okmulgee, Okmulgee County, Oklahoma; Coal Miner
Occupation: 1920 in Okmulgee, Okmulgee County, Oklahoma; Clerk in Loan Office
Occupation: 1930 in Oklahoma City, Oklahoma; Lease and Royalty Prosessor
Occupation: 1940 in Hugo, Choctaw County, Oklahoma; Independant Oil Lease Processor
Occupation: 1942 in Hugo, Choctaw County, Oklahoma; Self Employed
Occupation: 1949 in Hugo, Choctaw County, Oklahoma; Oil Lease Broker

More About Blanche Lee Hanlin:
Burial: Coalgate Cemetery, Coalgate, Oklahoma

Notes for Blanche Lee Hanlin:
Social Security death index gives year of death as 1963. Headstone gives year of death as 1962.

George Patterson Bell and Blanche Lee Hanlin had the following children:

1 EMMA DORIS[4] BELL was born in 1908 in Oklahoma. She died in 1979. She married Ray L. Primo about 1928. He was born in 1905 in Missouri. He died in 1956.

More About Emma Doris Bell:
Burial: Coalgate Cemetery, Coalgate, Oklahoma

2 WILLIAM BELL was born in Jan 1910 in Oklahoma.

11.   **ROBERT**[3] **PATTERSON** (William Kirkwood[2], Robert[1]) was born on 13 Dec 1882 in McAlester, Indian Territory (Present Day Oklahoma). He married **ANNIE WARD**. She was born about 1885 in Illinois.

More About Robert Patterson:
Occupation: 1900 in Coalgate, Choctaw Nation, Indian Territory (Present Day Oklahoma); Farm Labor
Occupation: 1920 in Murray, Coal County, Oklahoma; Coal Miner
Occupation: 1930 in Highland Park, Wayne County, Michigan; Service Man in Auto Industry
Occupation: 1940 in Schulter, Okmulgee County, Oklahoma; Coal Miner

Robert Patterson and Annie Ward had the following child:

   i.   HENZIE[4] PATTERSON was born about 1913 in Oklahoma. She married BILL LAYMOND.

12.   **MARY**[3] **PATTERSON** (William Kirkwood[2], Robert[1]) was born on 18 Feb 1885 in McAlester, Indian Territory (Present Day Oklahoma). She died in 1959. She married John Henderson Hall, son of John Henderson Hall and Jane Wallace on 25 Jan 1905 in Coalgate, Coal County, Choctaw Nation, Indian Territory (present day Oklahoma). He was born on 28 Jun 1881 in Bathgate, West Lothian, Scotland. He died in Nov 1967 in Oklahoma.

More About John Henderson Hall:
Living In: 1930 Sparta, Illinois
Occupation: 1900 in Coalgate, Choctaw Nation, Indian Territory (Present Day Oklahoma); Coal Miner
Occupation: 1940 in Schulter, Okmulgee County, Oklahoma; Coal Miner

John Henderson Hall and Mary Patterson had the following child:

   i.   ELIZABETH[4] HALL was born about 1907 in Oklahoma. She married JAMES LIDDELL. He was born about 1907 in Kansas. She married JOHN LEO GOUGH. He was born about 1906 in Oklahoma.

13.   **AGNES**[3] **PATTERSON** (William Kirkwood[2], Robert[1]) was born on 20 Mar 1895 in Coalgate, Indian Territory (Present Day Oklahoma). She married **CHARLES SOUTH**.

Charles South and Agnes Patterson had the following child:

   i.   CHARLES W.[4] SOUTH.

14.   **WILLIAM M.**[3] **PATTERSON** (William Kirkwood[2], Robert[1]) was born on 12 Dec 1898 in Dow, Indian Territory (Present Day Oklahoma). He married **LOUISE BELICK**.

More About William M. Patterson:
Occupation: 1920 in Murray, Coal County, Oklahoma; Coal Miner

William M. Patterson and Louise Belick had the following children:

   i.   BILLY[4] PATTERSON.

   ii.   GLORIA PATTERSON.

15.   **GILBERT**[3] **PATTERSON** (William Kirkwood[2], Robert[1]) was born on 26 Oct 1901 in Coalgate, Indian Territory (Present Day Oklahoma). He died on 18 Jun 1933 in Belleview, Illinois. He married Anna Adams on 26 Sep 1921 in Schulter, Oklahoma. She was born about 1904 in Ohio.

More About Gilbert Patterson:

Burial: 20 Jun 1933 in Caledonia Cemetery, Sparta, Illinois
Living In: 1920 With his parents in Murray, Coal County, Oklahoma
Occupation: 1920 in Murray, Coal County, Oklahoma; Automobile
Mechanic
Occupation: 1930 in Sparta, Illinois; Motion Picture Operator
Occupation: 1933 in Sparta, Illinois; Motion Picture Operator

More About Anna Adams:
Occupation: 1930 in Sparta, Illinois; Machine Operator in Rayon Factory

Gilbert Patterson and Anna Adams had the following children:

     i.   GILBERT[4] PATTERSON was born on 02 Jul 1922 in Sparta, Illinois.

          More About Gilbert Patterson:
          Military Service: Bet. 27 Jul 1942-14 Dec 1945; U.S. Navy, World War Two

     ii.   WILLIAM ROBERT PATTERSON was born about 1925 in Illinois.